Managing Editor
Ina Massler Levin, M.A.

Editor-in-Chief
Sharon Coan, M.S. Ed.

Illustrator
Sue Fullum

Cover Artist
Barb Lorseyedi

Art Coordinator
Kevin Barnes

Art Director
CJae Froshay

Imaging
Alfred Lau
James Edward Grace

Product Manager
Phil Garcia

Copyrighted materials and content reprinted with permission from Renaissance Corporate Services, Inc.

Publisher
Mary D. Smith, M.S. Ed.

Practice Makes Perfect
Reading Comprehension
GRADE 2

Author

Teacher Created Resources Staff

Teacher Created Resources, Inc.
6421 Industry Way
Westminster, CA 92683
www.teachercreated.com

ISBN: 978-0-7439-3332-2

©*2002 Teacher Created Resources, Inc.*
Reprinted, 2010
Made in U.S.A.

Table of Contents

Introduction 3

Fiction

    A Long Way to Travel 4

    Fire! 6

    The Great Sock Hunt 8

    On the Beach 10

    Growing Things 12

    Smiles 14

Nonfiction

    Bill Pickett 16

    Hanami—A Special Holiday 18

    Eclipses 20

    Salmon 22

    Clara Barton 24

    Snakes 26

Informational

    Butterfly Gardens 28

    Pumpkin Seeds 30

    Winter Fun 32

    At the Library 34

    The Hand Game 36

    Recipe for Giant Bubbles 38

Practice Tests

    Wondering—Fiction 40

    Osprey—Nonfiction 42

    Be a Rock Hound!—Informational 44

Answer Sheet 45

Answer Key 48

Introduction

The old adage "practice makes perfect" can really hold true for your child and his or her education. The more practice and exposure your child has with concepts being taught in school, the more success he or she is likely to find. For many parents, knowing how to help their children may be frustrating because the resources may not be readily available.

As a parent it is also difficult to know where to focus your efforts so that the extra practice your child receives at home supports what he or she is learning in school.

This book has been written to help parents and teachers reinforce basic skills with children. *Practice Makes Perfect: Reading Comprehension* gives practice in reading and answering questions to help fully comprehend what is read. The exercises in this book can be done sequentially or can be taken out of order, as needed.

After reading the story the questions can be answered either by circling the answers or by reproducing and using the fill-in answer sheets found on pages 46 and 47. The practice tests, one for each of the areas of reading, can be bubbled in on the answer pages that are provided for each test.

The following standards or objectives will be met or reinforced by completing the practice pages included in this book. These standards and objectives are similar to the ones required by your state and school district. These standards and objectives are appropriate for the second grade.

- The student will demonstrate competence in reading for understanding.
- The student will demonstrate competence in understanding how print is organized.
- The student will demonstrate competence in using various reading strategies to read the stories and answer the questions.
- The student will demonstrate competence in finding the main idea in a story, making inferences and making predictions.
- The student will demonstrate competence in beginning to recognize different types of reading (fiction, nonfiction, informational).

How to Make the Most of This Book

Here are some useful ideas for making the most of this book:

- Set aside a specific place in your home to work on this book. Keep it neat and tidy with materials ready on hand.
- Set up a certain time of day to work on these practice pages to establish consistency, or look for times in your day or week that are less hectic and conducive to practicing skills.
- Keep all practice sessions with your child positive and constructive. If the mood becomes frustrated or tense, set the book aside and look for another time to practice with your child. Forcing your child to perform will not help. Do not use this book as a punishment.
- Help beginning readers with instructions.
- Review the work your child has done.
- Allow the child to use whatever writing instruments he or she prefers. For example, colored pencils can add variety and pleasure to drill work.
- Pay attention to the areas in which your child has the most difficulty. Provide extra guidance and exercises in those areas.
- Read aloud with your child and ask reading comprehension questions.

A Long Way to Travel

Alex and his mother were walking on the beach one day after a storm.

"Look," Alex said. He pointed to a piece of round, blue glass almost covered with sand. They dug around it and found a round, glass ball. It was bigger than a softball, but smaller than a soccer ball.

"What is it?" Alex asked.

"It's a fisherman's float," his mother said. "I haven't seen one in years. Japanese fishermen once used to use them to keep their nets from sinking."

"Then this came all the way from Japan?" Alex asked. "Wow! It's traveled more than I have!"

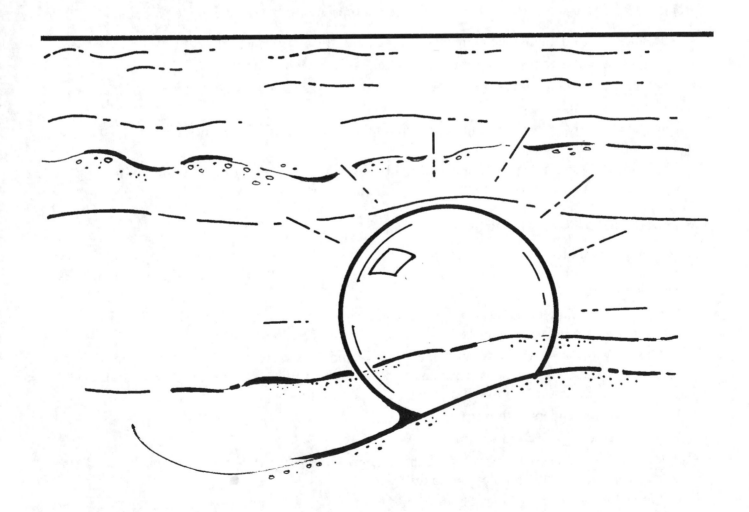

A Long Way to Travel *(cont.)*

Reading Comprehension Questions

After reading the story, answer the questions. Circle the correct answer.

1. Why did Alex say that the ball had traveled more than he had?
   a. Alex had never seen a fisherman's float before.
   b. Alex wanted to be a fisherman.
   c. Alex had probably never been to Japan.
   d. Alex and his mother travel a lot.

2. How did Alex probably feel at the end of the story?
   a. sad
   b. afraid
   c. excited
   d. tired

3. Which of these is a fact found in the story?
   a. Fisherman's floats are interesting.
   b. It is exciting to find things on the beach.
   c. Alex likes to travel.
   d. Japanese fisherman used floats.

4. What will probably happen next?
   a. A storm will send the float back to Japan.
   b. Alex will keep the fisherman's float.
   c. Alex will learn to fish, using the ball.
   d. Alex will take the ball back to Japan.

Fire!

When the fire alarm started to buzz, the class knew what to do. Brittany got in line and whispered to her friend Kelsey, "I wonder why we're having another fire drill. We already had one this week."

All the classes lined up on the playground. Then everyone turned and looked at the school. They were waiting for the "All Clear" bell to ring so they could go back inside.

But instead of the bell, they heard sirens! A huge fire truck raced up to the school! And then another one came! And right behind them were the police!

Everyone started whispering. And then Brittany heard, "Fire! It's a real fire!"

A real fire! Brittany felt very excited and very scared at the same time. Would their class burn down? What about Jason, their pet hamster?

Just then, the "All Clear" bell rang. The children looked at each other in surprise. Then they started back into the school.

"What happened?" they asked their teacher as soon as they were back inside.

"Oh," said their teacher. "One of the teachers was making toast, and it burned a little. The smoke set off the fire alarm."

Brittany whispered to Kelsey, "I'm glad it wasn't real. But it was exciting!"

Fire! *(cont.)*

Reading Comprehension Questions

After reading the story, answer the questions. Circle the correct answer.

1. Why did the fire alarm go off?

    a. It was time for a fire drill.

    b. The school was on fire.

    c. Some smoke from toast set it off.

    d. One of the students pulled the alarm.

2. Which of these events happened first?

    a. The students lined up on the playground.

    b. The fire alarm went off.

    c. The fire trucks came to the school.

    d. Brittany worried about Jason.

3. Why did the students think there was a real fire?

    a. They could smell the smoke.

    b. The fire alarm started to buzz.

    c. They had already had a fire drill that week.

    d. Firefighters and police came to the school.

4. When the "All Clear" bell rang, the students knew

    a. they should line up on the playground.

    b. there was no fire.

    c. there was no talking.

    d. school was out.

The Great Sock Hunt

Jenny never said that she had the neatest room in the world. But one day, she couldn't even find her socks. They were buried under piles of books, toys, and clothing.

"Let's have a Great Sock Hunt," her mother said. They hunted through the piles. The clothes went into a basket, the books went onto the shelves, and the toys went into the toy box. But all the socks were greeted with cheers and awarded points.

"I won!" Jenny cried at last. "I found six pairs! What's my prize?"

"A clean room," said her mother.

The Great Sock Hunt *(cont.)*

Reading Comprehension Questions

After reading the story, answer the questions. Circle the correct answer.

1. Why couldn't Jenny find her socks?

    a. She lost them at school.

    b. They were in a basket.

    c. Her room was messy.

    d. Her mom had hidden them.

2. How many socks did Jenny find?

    a. two

    b. eight

    c. four

    d. twelve

3. A lesson to be learned from the story is that

    a. socks are hard to find.

    b. your mom should help you clean your room.

    c. when your room is clean, you can find what you need.

    d. your room is more fun when it is messy.

4. Why did Jenny clean her room?

    a. Her mother turned it into a game.

    b. She wanted the neatest room in the world.

    c. She was tired of it being messy.

    d. She wanted to get her books on shelves.

On the Beach

Carlos and Merry often went to the beach. Carlos liked to pick up shells, and Merry enjoyed watching the birds.

But one day the children found something very different. Carlos saw it first because he was looking at the sand.

"Merry," said Carlos, "Come here quickly!"

Merry stopped watching the seagulls dive and swoop. She ran over to Carlos. He was looking at a long, brown-gray, fishy kind of animal.

"What is it?" asked Merry.

"I think it's a small shark," said Carlos.

Merry looked at the sharp teeth and pointy fins. She said, "I think you're right."

"Is it still alive?" asked Carlos.

"No," answered Merry. "Sharks can't live out of water."

The children looked at the shark a long time. Finally, Carlos said, "Let's go home. I want to tell Mother what we found on the beach!"

On the Beach *(cont.)*

Reading Comprehension Questions

After reading the story, answer the questions. Circle the correct answer.

1. Where did Carlos and Merry find the "fishy kind of animal"?
    a. in the water
    b. in the sand
    c. next to some birds
    d. by a sea shell

2. Why did Carlos want to go home?
    a. He was tired.
    b. He was scared.
    c. He wanted to tell his mom what they found.
    d. He wanted to wash his new shells.

3. The children knew the fish was a shark because it
    a. tried to bite Merry.
    b. had come from the water.
    c. was long, brown-gray, and fishy.
    d. had sharp teeth and pointy fins.

4. You can tell from the story that Carlos and Merry
    a. find a lot of dead things.
    b. enjoy going to the beach.
    c. see sharks often.
    d. like sharks.

Growing Things

It was a sunny day, and Tory was digging in his garden. He had a special box just for tomatoes, but right now he was watering his sunflowers. They were very tall, taller than Tory. Each sunflower had bright yellow petals. The sunflowers grew straight to the sky, except one. One sunflower leaned over the fence as if to talk to Tory's dog, Lia.

Lia barked at the sunflower, but the sunflower didn't answer. Lia barked again, then sat down. Tory put down his watering can and opened the gate.

"Okay, Lia," he said, "The flower won't talk to you, but I will. Time to play."

Lia wagged her tail in happiness.

Growing Things *(cont.)*

Reading Comprehension Questions

After reading the story, answer the questions. Circle the correct answer.

1. The next thing that will probably happen is that
    a. Lia will bark at the tomatoes.
    b. Tory and Lia will play.
    c. Tory will water his sunflowers.
    d. Tory will water his tomatoes.

2. The best way to find out more about sunflowers is to
    a. ask your teacher.
    b. read a book about garden flowers.
    c. read a made-up story about a garden.
    d. look in today's newspaper.

3. Why did Lia bark at the sunflower?
    a. She wanted to go into the garden.
    b. She thought it would talk to her.
    c. It was leaning over the fence.
    d. She was afraid of it.

4. What do these words mean: The sunflowers grew straight to the sky?
    a. The flowers were leaning over.
    b. The flowers were touching the sky.
    c. The flowers were taller than Tory.
    d. The flowers grew straight up.

Smiles

"Smile," said the woman with the camera.

Teddy didn't feel like smiling. He was sad because his puppy was lost. The woman with the camera took his picture anyway.

"Next," she said.

Teddy jumped off the stool and his friend Harriet climbed up. The woman with the camera was taking pictures of everybody in Mr. Jenkins's class. Teddy waited until Harriet was done. Then they walked outdoors.

"What's that?" asked Harriet, pointing toward the sidewalk.

"Curly!" cried Teddy. His puppy had followed him to school!

Teddy couldn't stop smiling for the rest of the day.

Smiles *(cont.)*

Reading Comprehension Questions

After reading the story answer the questions. Circle the correct answer.

1. From the story, you can tell that Teddy
    a. likes having his picture taken.
    b. likes his dog a lot.
    c. does not like to smile.
    d. does not like Mr. Jenkins.

2. Why did Teddy walk outdoors?
    a. He wanted to find his puppy.
    b. He and Harriet were done getting their picture taken.
    c. He wanted to go outside and play.
    d. He wanted to get away from the woman with the camera.

3. What was the name of Teddy's puppy?
    a. Jenkins
    b. Curly
    c. Teddy
    d. Harriet

4. This story could not be called
    a. "Curly, Gets His Picture Taken."
    b. "Teddy's Bad Day."
    c. "Picture Day."
    d. "Where Is Curly?"

5. How did Teddy feel at the end of the story?
    a. happy
    b. sad
    c. scared
    d. angry

Bill Pickett

One of the most famous rodeo performers was Bill Pickett. Born in 1870, he was only ten years old when he began working as a cowboy. He was one of the best steer wrestlers ever.

Steer wrestling isn't easy. You have to gallop next to a large bull, then jump off and grab it by the horns. Then, you have to stop the bull, and get it to lie down on the ground, all within ten seconds.

Some say Bill Pickett invented steer wrestling. He certainly made the event famous as he toured the country, showing off his skill.

Bill Pickett *(cont.)*

Reading Comprehension Questions

After reading the story, answer the questions. Circle the correct answer.

1. You can tell that steer wrestling is
    a. hard.
    b. safe.
    c. silly.
    d. easy.

2. This story is mostly about
    a. a famous horse.
    b. a famous cowboy.
    c. an exciting rodeo.
    d. a rodeo clown.

3. You could probably find this story in a book called
    a. *How to Be a Cowboy.*
    b. *Bulls are Big.*
    c. *Hard Working Steers.*
    d. *Famous Rodeo People.*

4. You are wrestling a steer. You have stopped it. What do you do next?
    a. Get it to lie down.
    b. Gallop next to it.
    c. Ride it for 2 minutes.
    d. Grab it by the horns.

5. What would a rodeo performer do?
    a. buy bulls for the rodeo
    b. get a bull ready for the rodeo
    c. feed and care for the steers
    d. wrestle a steer or ride a bull

Hanami — A Special Holiday

In Japan, the cherry blossom is special. Its soft, pink blossoms make people think about nature. The cherry blossoms last only for a few days each year. But, when they are in bloom, the slightest breeze will send their petals drifting through the air like snow.

When the trees are in bloom, people in Japan celebrate Hanami (cherry blossom viewing). They hold parties under the trees in the evening. This tradition dates from long ago, when poets would gather under the trees and read poems about their beautiful cherry blossoms.

Hanami — A Special Holiday *(cont.)*

Reading Comprehension Questions

After reading the story, answer the questions. Circle the correct answer.

1. This story could also be called
   a. "Cherry Blossom Holiday."
   b. "The History of Japan."
   c. "Pink Parties."
   d. "Japanese Poems."

2. In Japan, cherry blossoms are
   a. important.
   b. long-lasting.
   c. ugly.
   d. yellow.

3. During Hanami, the people of Japan hold parties
   a. in the snow, at night.
   b. under cherry trees, in the snow.
   c. under cherry trees, at night.
   d. under cherry trees from long ago.

4. The best way to find out more about cherry blossoms is to
   a. eat some cherries.
   b. look up cherry blossoms in the library.
   c. go to Japan.
   d. draw a picture of a cherry blossom.

5. Why do people in Japan think cherry blossoms are special?
   a. The people who live in Japan like snow.
   b. Cherry blossoms make people think about nature.
   c. There are no other holidays in Japan.
   d. There are many poems about cherry blossoms.

Eclipses

Most of the time, we see the moon at night and the sun during the day. But every once in a while, the moon passes directly in front of the sun, blocking its light. When this happens, the moon's shadow falls on the earth, and suddenly the sky grows dark. This is called a solar eclipse.

You have to be in just the right place to see a solar eclipse. The shadow of the moon is only 200 miles wide by the time it reaches the earth. But for those people lucky enough to see it, an eclipse is a wonderful sight.

Eclipses *(cont.)*

Reading Comprehension Questions

After reading the story, answer the questions. Circle the correct answer.

1. What is a solar eclipse?
   a. the moon during the daytime
   b. the earth's shadow on the moon
   c. the sun's shadow on the moon
   d. the moon's shadow on the earth

2. During an eclipse, the sky grows dark because
   a. it always rains during eclipses.
   b. day is turning into night.
   c. the moon is blocking the light from the sun.
   d. we can only see the moon at night.

3. You have to be lucky to see an eclipse because
   a. you have to be in just the right place.
   b. the sun hides the eclipse from the earth.
   c. you would be able to see the sun in the daytime.
   d. it only happens every 200 years.

4. To find out more about eclipses, you could read a book called
   a. All About the Earth We Live On.
   b. The Day the Cow Jumped Over the Moon.
   c. Why the Moon Never Talks to the Sun.
   d. All About the Sun and Moon

5. Most of the time we see the moon
   a. at night.
   b. during the day.
   c. when it is cold.
   d. at noon.

Salmon

Salmon are fish that are born in freshwater streams. When they are old enough, they swim down the rivers to the ocean, which is made of salt water. After years in the ocean, salmon return to the streams where they were born. There, they lay eggs for new salmon.

It is easy for the young salmon to reach the ocean because the rivers flow in that direction. Coming back is much harder. The salmon have to swim against the current. They might have to jump up rapids and waterfalls. Only a small number of salmon ever make it back home.

Salmon *(cont.)*

Reading Comprehension Questions

After reading the story, answer the questions. Circle the correct answer.

1. Why do only a small number of salmon make it back home?
   a. Salmon are very slow swimmers.
   b. Salmon like salt water better than fresh water.
   c. Salmon are not old enough to make it back home.
   d. Salmon have to swim against the current coming home.

2. Where are salmon born?
   a. in freshwater streams
   b. in salt water
   c. in waterfalls
   d. in the ocean

3. The reason salmon swim back home is to
   a. lay their eggs.
   b. jump up rapids.
   c. drink fresh water.
   d. visit their families.

4. In this story, the word *streams* means
   a. groups of salmon.
   b. tails on jets.
   c. loud sounds.
   d. bodies of running water.

5. Rivers flow in
   a. one direction.
   b. two directions.
   c. three directions.
   d. four directions.

Clara Barton

Clara Barton always did her best to help people. She got medical supplies to the army doctors during the Civil War. She nursed soldiers in the battlefield, no matter which side they were on. She spent hours looking for missing and hurt men.

After the war was over, she started the American National Red Cross. This is a group that helps people during floods, fires, and other disasters. Because of her efforts, the Red Cross has helped thousands of people during times of need.

Clara Barton *(cont.)*

Reading Comprehension Questions

After reading the story, answer the questions. Circle the correct answer.

1. In this story, the word *disasters* means
   a. the Civil War.
   b. terrible happenings, like fires and floods.
   c. battlefields where wars are fought.
   d. missing and hurt men.

2. Clara Barton probably believed that
   a. people only need help after a flood or fire.
   b. you should help your friends, but not your enemies.
   c. you should help people whenever they need help.
   d. the Red Cross should help win wars.

3. When did Clara Barton start the Red Cross?
   a. during the Civil War
   b. after the Civil War
   c. during a flood
   d. after some disasters

4. The word *efforts* means
   a. war.
   b. work.
   c. soldier.
   d. group.

5. Why did Clara Barton look for missing and hurt men?
   a. so that they could take supplies to the army doctors
   b. so that they could join the Red Cross
   c. so that she could take care of them
   d. so that they could fight in the war again

Snakes

Have you ever held a snake? Did you think it would feel slimy?

Snakes are not slimy. If they are healthy, they are dry and smooth. Their bodies are covered with scales. Even their eyes are covered with see-through scales instead of eyelids.

Snakes can swim, climb a tree, crawl along ropes, and slither along the ground. The Western Whip Snake is one of the fastest snakes. It can travel up to three miles an hour.

Snakes are cold-blooded, and most snakes sleep through the winter. All snakes swallow their food whole and shed their skin when it gets too tight.

Snakes don't hear, but they feel sounds with their bodies. Snakes taste and smell with their tongues.

What do you suppose a snake thinks we feel like?

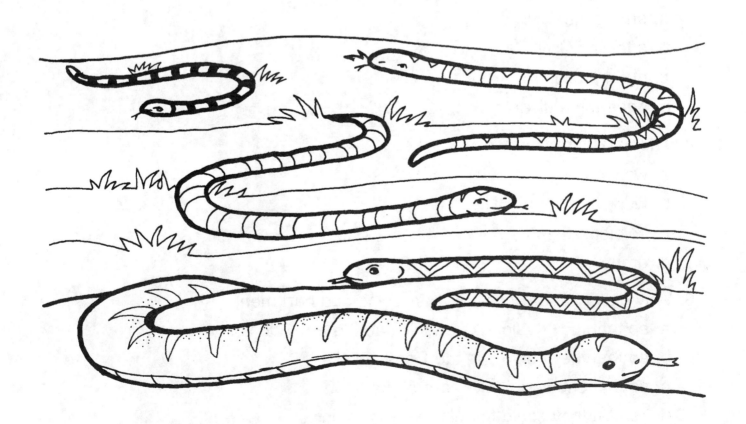

Snakes *(cont.)*

Reading Comprehension Questions

After reading the story, answer the questions. Circle the correct answer.

1. Snakes have see-through scales over their eyes
   a. because they can't hear.
   b. to keep their eyes safe.
   c. so they can see better.
   d. to scare people.

2. What kind of story is this?
   a. poem
   b. true story
   c. fairy tale
   d. fiction

3. If a snake is dry and smooth, it is
   a. sick.
   b. sleeping.
   c. about to bite.
   d. healthy.

4. Why do snakes shed their skin?
   a. to get rid of a skin that's too small
   b. to protect themselves
   c. to change colors so they can blend in
   d. to keep them from getting sick

5. Snakes feel sounds with their
   a. ears.
   b. tongues
   c. bodies.
   d. eyes.

Butterfly Gardens

If you like butterflies, you can create a garden for them to visit.

Things you will need: a sunny place to plant things, seeds or seedlings, and a shallow dish of water.

First: Choose a sunny place with little or no wind.

Second: Pick flowers to plant. Butterflies like pink and white flowers with broad, flat blossoms.

Third: Plant the flowers in your garden.

Fourth: Put the shallow dish near the flowers and keep it filled with water. Butterflies need water.

Follow these steps, and you may find your garden filled with bright, beautiful butterflies through the summer.

Butterfly Gardens *(cont.)*

Reading Comprehension Questions

After reading the story, answer the questions. Circle the correct answer

1. What is the third step?
    a. Fill the dish with water.
    b. Plant the flowers.
    c. Pick some flowers.
    d. Choose a sunny place.

2. The word *seedling* means a
    a. shallow dish.
    b. flat blossom.
    c. young plant.
    d. sunny place.

3. This story is mostly about
    a. sunny places with no wind.
    b. keeping butterflies as pets.
    c. making a butterfly garden.
    d. making a flower garden.

4. A book with more ideas like this could be called
    a. *Flowers for Your Garden.*
    b. *Get a Butterfly to Visit You.*
    c. *Billy Butterfly and the Big Brown Bear.*
    d. *Planting Your Garden.*

5. Butterflies may visit your garden in the month of
    a. February.
    b. July.
    c. January.
    d. December.

Pumpkin Seeds

Here is a fun recipe for toasted pumpkin seeds. Have an adult help you with the oven.

You need:

one large pumpkin

one teaspoon salt

Scoop the seeds out of the pumpkin. Separate the seeds from the pulp (you may need to pick some out by hand). Rinse the seeds. Spread the seeds on a cookie sheet. Sprinkle them with the salt.

Toast the seeds at 350°F. After a few minutes, turn the seeds over. When they are just golden, take them out. They are good to eat warm or cold.

Pumpkin Seeds *(cont.)*

Reading Comprehension Questions

After reading the story answer the questions. Circle the correct answer

1. You could probably find this recipe in a
   a. storybook.
   b. cookbook about desserts.
   c. book of poems.
   d. cookbook about snacks.

2. You should take the seeds out of the oven
   a. to sprinkle them with salt.
   b. before you rinse them.
   c. before they turn golden.
   d. when they are golden.

3. The seeds should toast
   a. for 350 minutes.
   b. until they are warm.
   c. for one hour.
   d. for a few minutes.

4. Why should you ask an adult to help you with the oven?
   a. Ovens can be dangerous.
   b. It is easy to burn pumpkin seeds.
   c. It is hard to set an oven to the correct temperature.
   d. You should use a toaster instead of an oven.

5. The word *separate* means
   a. turn over.
   b. move apart.
   c. mix together.
   d. sprinkle.

Winter Fun

When snow falls, nothing is more fun than building a snowperson.

Step 1: Start by making a snowball. Roll it on the ground until it is about two feet round.

Step 2: Make another, slightly smaller ball for the body. Get a friend to help you lift it onto the first ball.

Step 3: Pack snow in between the two balls to keep the top one from falling off.

Step 4: Make a third, even smaller ball for the head. Place it on the second ball and pack it with snow.

Step 5: Decorate your snow person with pebbles, buttons, carrot noses, and an old hat and scarf!

Winter Fun <small>(cont.)</small>

Reading Comprehension Questions A

After reading the story, answer the questions. Circle the correct answer.

1. In the story, the words *When snow falls* mean
   a. when you get snow down your clothes and shoes.
   b. when you fall down trying to walk in the snow.
   c. when it snows in the winter.
   d. when snow falls off the trees and houses.

2. You should decorate your snow person with
   a. extra snow to keep it from falling apart.
   b. things you find around your house.
   c. some new clothes from the store.
   d. crayons, paint, or chalk.

3. The smallest ball is used for
   a. snowball fights.
   b. the head.
   c. the body.
   d. decorations.

4. This story was probably written to tell you
   a. why snowpeople are important.
   b. one way to have fun with snow.
   c. how to recycle things like old hats.
   d. why you need a friend in the winter.

5. You will need help in step
   a. five.
   b. two.
   c. one.
   d. four.

At the Library

Welcome! The library is your gateway to fun and facts, to new faces and new places! Please ask for help from any librarian whenever you need it.

- Please don't eat or drink in the library. And please be quiet because others are reading and studying.

- To check out books, videos, CDs, and tapes, you need a library card. To get a library card, you need to:

  1. ask a librarian for a library card form

  2. fill out the form

  3. ask your parent or guardian to sign it

  4. give the finished form to any librarian

- Then you will get your own library card! You will have your very own key to all the new worlds to be found in the library.

At the Library *(cont.)*

Reading Comprehension Questions

After reading the story, answer the questions. Circle the correct answer.

1. Why should you be quiet in the library?

    a. So you can hear your friends talk to you.

    b. So people can listen to the music.

    c. So you don't bother the librarians.

    d. So you don't bother others who are reading.

2. You should ask for help from

    a. someone who doesn't look busy.

    b. one of the librarians.

    c. someone who looks smart.

    d. the person next to you.

3. A librarian is a person who

    a. reads all the books in the library.

    b. keeps the books safe.

    c. helps people use the library.

    d. cleans the library.

4. How does the writer feel about the library?

    a. Libraries are full of information.

    b. Libraries are mostly for grown-ups.

    c. Libraries can be hard to use.

    d. Libraries are quiet, and there is nothing to do.

5. What can be checked out?

    a. books, papers, DVDs, CDs

    b. forms, cards tapes,

    c. toys, boxes, tapes, CDs

    d. books, videos, CDs, tapes

The Hand Game

Here is a game you can play anytime, anywhere, with anyone. All you need are two small stones and some red paint. Paint a red dot on one of the stones, and you are ready to play.

How to Play:

1. Sit in a circle with the other players.

2. Hold both stones in one hand.

3. Pass one stone to a person near you without letting anyone see it.

4. Ask another person to guess which stone you passed. Was it the one with the red dot, or the other one?

5. If this person guesses correctly, give him both stones. Now it is that person's turn.

6. If he doesn't guess correctly, give the stones to someone else.

7. Play the game again.

8. Whoever guesses correctly the most times wins.

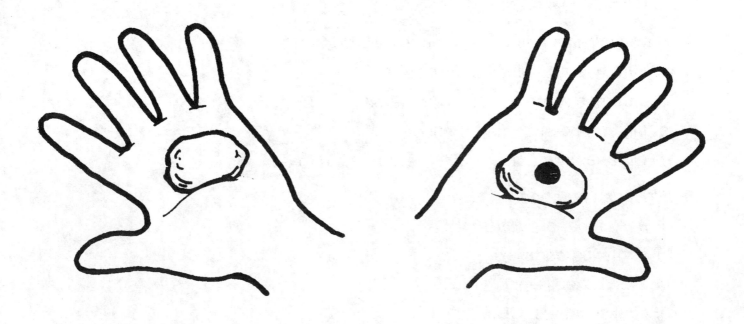

The Hand Game

Reading Comprehension Questions

After reading the story answer the questions. Circle the correct answer.

1. The game would not be fair if
   a. there was a blue dot on the stone instead of a red dot.
   b. you didn't sit in a circle.
   c. you used big stones instead of little stones
   d. there were no dots on the stones.

2. You could probably find this game in a book called
   a. *Games You Can Make.*
   b. *How To Trick Your Friends.*
   c. *How To Paint.*
   d. *All About Stones.*

3. What happens if the person guesses correctly?
   a. She loses her next turn.
   b. She gets to paint the stones.
   c. She gets both the stones.
   d. She gets to leave the circle.

4. How old do you have to be to play this game?
   a. any age
   b. over 8
   c. under 15
   d. over 4

5. What is another good name for this game?
   a. One Dot, Two Dot, Red Dot, Blue Dot
   b. Stones and Paint
   c. Hot Stones
   d. Guess the Dot

Recipe for Giant Bubbles

Here is a great game for a hot day. You should have everything you need around your home.

You will need:

dishpan or cookie sheet

water

dish soap

wire hangers

1. Fill the dishpan or cookie sheet with warm water and dish soap and mix well.

2. Make bubble wands by bending each wire hanger into any shape you like. You could make a circle, or an oval, or even a diamond. Straighten the hooked end into a handle.

3. Dip your wand into the bubble mixture and wave it around in the air. You should have giant bubbles!

Recipe for Giant Bubbles *(cont.)*

Reading Comprehension Questions

After reading the story, answer the questions. Circle the correct answer.

1. According to the story, making giant bubbles is a good thing to do
   a. during the summer.
   b. at a dress-up party.
   c. at school, during recess.
   d. during the winter.

2. What is the second step in the instructions?
   a. Make a bubble wand out of a hanger.
   b. Wash the dishpan or cookie sheet.
   c. Dip the wand into the bubble mixture.
   d. Fill a dishpan or cookie sheet with warm water.

3. How many different things will you need to make Giant Bubbles?
   a. seven
   b. six
   c. four
   d. three

4. The best way to answer the question right before this one is to
   a. guess the number of things you will need.
   b. imagine that you are making the bubbles.
   c. count the number of things on the "you will need" list
   d. count the number of steps in the instructions.

5. In this story, a *wand* is something that
   a. makes magic.
   b. is used to hang up clothes.
   c. creates a popping noise.
   d. makes bubbles.

> **Directions:** Read this story carefully. When you are completely finished answer the questions on the next page. Make sure to bubble in your answers completely.

Wondering

Dane looked at the canoe. It was still upside down on the dock. Where was Aunt Lyn? She had promised to take him canoeing today.

There she was—but what did she have in her hands? Her arms were full of a big basket and some other things. Dane wondered what they were.

"Here, Dane, put this on." Aunt Lyn handed him a puffy orange life vest. She watched while Dane buckled all the straps.

"Is it too loose?" she asked. Dane shook his head.

"Is it too tight?" Dane shook his head, no, again.

"Good," said Aunt Lyn. She strapped on her own purple life vest. Together they rolled the canoe over into the water. Then Aunt Lyn put the big basket into the canoe.

As they moved downstream, Dane wondered what was in the picnic basket!

Wondering *(cont.)*

Reading Comprehension Test Questions

1. You can tell from the story that
   - (a) Aunt Lyn is a good cook.
   - (b) Aunt Lyn believes in being safe.
   - (c) Dane is afraid of going canoeing.
   - (d) Dane is angry with his Aunt Lyn.

2. Why was Dane waiting for Aunt Lyn?
   - (a) She was supposed to take Dane home.
   - (b) She was supposed to take Dane canoeing.
   - (c) She was supposed to take Dane on a picnic.
   - (d) She was supposed to bring life vests.

3. What color was Aunt Lyn's life vest?
   - (a) orange
   - (b) blue
   - (c) yellow
   - (d) purple

4. In this story, what does the word *buckled* mean?
   - (a) folded
   - (b) bent
   - (c) fastened
   - (d) bumped

5. Why did Dane and Aunt Lyn roll the canoe over?
   - (a) To put it in the water.
   - (b) To admire it.
   - (c) To move it upstream.
   - (d) To have fun together.

Directions: Read this story carefully. When you are completely finished answer the questions on the next page. Make sure to bubble in your answers completely.

Osprey

You probably know that some birds can fish. But did you know that there is a bird that fishes with its feet?

An osprey is a bird that is bigger than a robin, but smaller than an eagle. It has dark feathers on most of its back, white belly feathers, and a white head. The female osprey has dark streaks and spots around her neck, but the male does not. His neck is all white.

When they fly, osprey wings are slightly bent back like a seagull's. They glide high in the air like a hawk. Ospreys like to nest near fresh and salt water. They dive for fish and catch them—with their feet!

Osprey *(cont.)*

Reading Comprehension Test Questions

1. This story was written mainly to
   - (a) tell you how ospreys are like hawks.
   - (b) tell you about the osprey.
   - (c) show how ospreys have changed.
   - (d) tell that an osprey is bigger than a robin.

2. The osprey uses its feet to
   - (a) pick up sticks.
   - (b) fly over water.
   - (c) walk on the water.
   - (d) catch fish.

3. How is an osprey like a seagull?
   - (a) It flies with its wings bent back.
   - (b) It fishes with its feet.
   - (c) It has spots.
   - (d) It glides high in the air.

4. Why do ospreys like to nest near fresh and salt water?
   - (a) They get their food from the water.
   - (b) They like to take baths every day.
   - (c) They are bigger than robins.
   - (d) They have white belly feathers.

5. In this story, what does the word slightly mean?
   - (a) quite a bit
   - (b) straight
   - (c) a little bit
   - (d) completely

> **Directions:** Read this story carefully. When you are completely finished answer the questions on the next page. Make sure to bubble in your answers completely

Be a Rock Hound!

Rock hounds are people who like to collect rocks. To get the most out of a rock-collecting trip, you should wear comfortable clothes and shoes. Put on sunscreen or wear a hat. You should also bring:

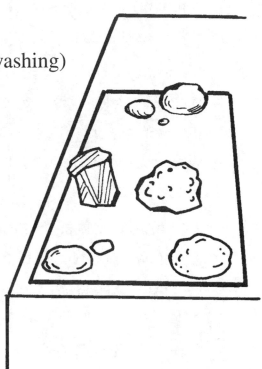

1. a raincoat

2. a water bottle (for drinking and for rock washing)

3. a first-aid kit

4. a map and a compass

5. a whistle

6. gloves

7. tools (rock hammer, shovel, pickax)

8. containers for special or small rocks

9. a backpack to put everything in

10. good common sense!

Many people have rock collections that they have added to and enjoyed their whole lifetime. Why don't you join them?

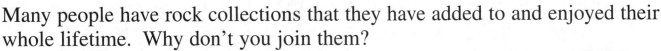

Be a Rock Hound! *(cont.)*

Reading Comprehension Test Questions

1. The best way to learn more about rock collecting would be to
   - (a) study a lot of rocks.
   - (b) wear a raincoat to collect rocks.
   - (c) read the story again.
   - (d) put rocks in your garden.

2. Rock hounds are
   - (a) dogs who are good at climbing over rocky places.
   - (b) people who enjoy collecting rocks.
   - (c) dogs trained to find special rocks.
   - (d) people who like both dogs and rocks.

3. The writer probably believes that rock collecting
   - (a) is hard to do.
   - (b) can be boring.
   - (c) is mostly for grownups.
   - (d) is a fun hobby.

4. When you go rock collecting, you should bring a backpack with you because
   - (a) you need something to put everything in.
   - (b) you need to protect your back from the sun.
   - (c) you should bring homework with you.
   - (d) you should go rock collecting after school.

5. Why should you bring a whistle?
   - (a) to make bird calls so you can see new birds
   - (b) to call your rock hound in case he runs away
   - (c) to have something to play with while you rest
   - (d) to get attention in case you get lost

Answer Sheet

This sheet may be reproduced and use with the reading comprehension questions. Each box can be used with one story. Using the answer sheets with the stories and questions gives extra practice in test preparation.

Page 5	Page 7	Page 9
1. (a) (b) (c) (d)	1. (a) (b) (c) (d)	1. (a) (b) (c) (d)
2. (a) (b) (c) (d)	2. (a) (b) (c) (d)	2. (a) (b) (c) (d)
3. (a) (b) (c) (d)	3. (a) (b) (c) (d)	3. (a) (b) (c) (d)
4. (a) (b) (c) (d)	4. (a) (b) (c) (d)	4. (a) (b) (c) (d)

Page 11	Page 13	Page 15
1. (a) (b) (c) (d)	1. (a) (b) (c) (d)	1. (a) (b) (c) (d)
2. (a) (b) (c) (d)	2. (a) (b) (c) (d)	2. (a) (b) (c) (d)
3. (a) (b) (c) (d)	3. (a) (b) (c) (d)	3. (a) (b) (c) (d)
4. (a) (b) (c) (d)	4. (a) (b) (c) (d)	4. (a) (b) (c) (d)
		5. (a) (b) (c) (d)

Page 17	Page 19	Page 21
1. (a) (b) (c) (d)	1. (a) (b) (c) (d)	1. (a) (b) (c) (d)
2. (a) (b) (c) (d)	2. (a) (b) (c) (d)	2. (a) (b) (c) (d)
3. (a) (b) (c) (d)	3. (a) (b) (c) (d)	3. (a) (b) (c) (d)
4. (a) (b) (c) (d)	4. (a) (b) (c) (d)	4. (a) (b) (c) (d)
5. (a) (b) (c) (d)	5. (a) (b) (c) (d)	5. (a) (b) (c) (d)

Answer Sheet *(cont.)*

Page 23	Page 25	Page 27
1. ⓐ ⓑ ⓒ ⓓ	1. ⓐ ⓑ ⓒ ⓓ	1. ⓐ ⓑ ⓒ ⓓ
2. ⓐ ⓑ ⓒ ⓓ	2. ⓐ ⓑ ⓒ ⓓ	2. ⓐ ⓑ ⓒ ⓓ
3. ⓐ ⓑ ⓒ ⓓ	3. ⓐ ⓑ ⓒ ⓓ	3. ⓐ ⓑ ⓒ ⓓ
4. ⓐ ⓑ ⓒ ⓓ	4. ⓐ ⓑ ⓒ ⓓ	4. ⓐ ⓑ ⓒ ⓓ
5. ⓐ ⓑ ⓒ ⓓ	5. ⓐ ⓑ ⓒ ⓓ	5. ⓐ ⓑ ⓒ ⓓ

Page 29	Page 31	Page 33
1. ⓐ ⓑ ⓒ ⓓ	1. ⓐ ⓑ ⓒ ⓓ	1. ⓐ ⓑ ⓒ ⓓ
2. ⓐ ⓑ ⓒ ⓓ	2. ⓐ ⓑ ⓒ ⓓ	2. ⓐ ⓑ ⓒ ⓓ
3. ⓐ ⓑ ⓒ ⓓ	3. ⓐ ⓑ ⓒ ⓓ	3. ⓐ ⓑ ⓒ ⓓ
4. ⓐ ⓑ ⓒ ⓓ	4. ⓐ ⓑ ⓒ ⓓ	4. ⓐ ⓑ ⓒ ⓓ
5. ⓐ ⓑ ⓒ ⓓ	5. ⓐ ⓑ ⓒ ⓓ	5. ⓐ ⓑ ⓒ ⓓ

Page 35	Page 37	Page 39
1. ⓐ ⓑ ⓒ ⓓ	1. ⓐ ⓑ ⓒ ⓓ	1. ⓐ ⓑ ⓒ ⓓ
2. ⓐ ⓑ ⓒ ⓓ	2. ⓐ ⓑ ⓒ ⓓ	2. ⓐ ⓑ ⓒ ⓓ
3. ⓐ ⓑ ⓒ ⓓ	3. ⓐ ⓑ ⓒ ⓓ	3. ⓐ ⓑ ⓒ ⓓ
4. ⓐ ⓑ ⓒ ⓓ	4. ⓐ ⓑ ⓒ ⓓ	4. ⓐ ⓑ ⓒ ⓓ
5. ⓐ ⓑ ⓒ ⓓ	5. ⓐ ⓑ ⓒ ⓓ	5. ⓐ ⓑ ⓒ ⓓ

Answer Key

A Long Way to Travel, page 5
1. c
2. c
3. d
4. b

Fire, page 7
1. c
2. b
3. d
4. b

The Great Sock Hunt, page 9
1. c
2. d
3. c
4. a

On the Beach, page 11
1. b
2. c
3. d
4. b

Growing Things, page 13
1. b
2. b
3. c or b
4. d

Smiles, page 15
1. b
2. b
3. b
4. a
5. a

Bill Pickett, page 17
1. a
2. b
3. d
4. a
5. d

Hanami—A Special Holiday, page 19
1. a
2. a
3. c
4. b
5. b

Eclipses, page 21
1. d
2. c
3. a
4. d
5. a

Salmon, page 23
1. d
2. a
3. a
4. d
5. a

Clara Barton, page 25
1. b
2. c
3. b
4. b
5. c

Snakes, page 27
1. b
2. b
3. d
4. a
5. c

Butterfly Gardens, page 29
1. b
2. c
3. c
4. b
5. b

Pumpkin Seeds, page 31
1. d
2. d
3. d
4. a
5. b

Winter Fun, page 33
1. c
2. b
3. b
4. b
5. b

At the Library, page 35
1. d
2. b
3. c
4. a
5. d

The Hand Game, page 37
1. d
2. a
3. c
4. a
5. d

Recipe for Giant Bubbles, page 39
1. a
2. a
3. c
4. c
5. d

Wondering, page 41
1. b
2. b
3. d
4. c
5. a

Osprey, page 43
1. b
2. d
3. a
4. a
5. c

Be a Rock Hound!, page 45
1. a
2. b
3. d
4. a
5. d